STRANDED AT SEA

Ellen Linnihan

SADDLEBACK
EDUCATIONAL PUBLISHING

ASTONISHING HEADLINES

Attacked

Captured

Condemned

Kidnapped

Lost and Found

Missing

Shot Down

Stowed Away

Stranded at Sea

Trapped

SADDLEBACK
EDUCATIONAL PUBLISHING
www.sdlback.com

ISBN-13: 978-1-61651-926-1
ISBN-10: 1-61651-926-6
eBook: 978-1-61247-083-2

Printed in Guangzhou, China
NOR/0814/CA21401313

18 17 16 15 14   2 3 4 5 6

Photo Credits: Cover, page 51, Corbis; page 34, Picture History; page 39, 43, 47, United Holocaust Memorial Museum; pages 64–65, Gallo Images / Getty Images News / Getty Images; pages 76–77, Handout / Getty Images News / Getty Images; pages 84–85, © Canettistock | Dreamstime.com

CONTENTS

The sea is a deadly place.

Whether you are an experienced sailor or a child on a raft, the ocean shows no mercy. Above the surface, the deadly forces are great. Sea storms split the greatest ships in half. The water, so vast and cool, defies human thirst. Salty seawater makes you thirsty if you drink it.

The sun beats without mercy upon sailors. It strips the moisture from helpless bodies. It burns and dehydrates while the sea offers no shade.

On the sea's surface, pirates roam, searching for victims and treasure. There are few witnesses to the mutinies and murders.

Icebergs haunt the Arctic and Antarctic waters. Their razor-sharp edges can slice a ship and send her to the bottom of the sea.

The creatures of the sea prey on the helpless humans who dare to brave the waters. The sharks are hungry for blood.

Below the sea's surface lurk unseen human enemies. During war, submarines torpedo unsuspecting ships.

Many with great skill and knowledge have lost their lives while stranded at sea. Survival is a gift.

Mutiny on the High Seas
DATAFILE

Timeline

December 1787

HMS *Bounty* sets sail from Spithead, England, bound for Tahiti.

April 1789

Fletcher Christian leads a mutiny against Captain William Bligh. They set Bligh and 17 men adrift in a small boat.

Where Did Captain Bligh Sail?

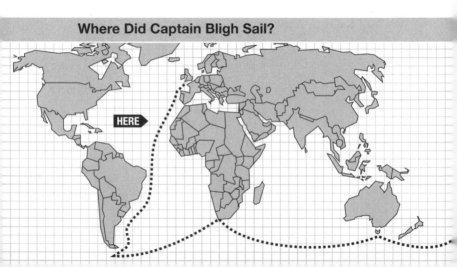

Key Terms

breadfruit—a seedless, starchy fruit that looks and tastes like bread

mutiny—an effort to overthrow a leader

ration—to limit the daily amount of food allowed for each person

replica—a copy or model of something

sauerkraut—cooked and pickled cabbage

scurvy—a disease caused by lack of ascorbic acid, often found in fruit

?

Did You Know?

Every year on January 23, the Pitcairn Islanders celebrate Bounty Day by setting fire to a replica of the HMS *Bounty*. Today, 50 people live on Pitcairn Island. Only a few are not the mutineers' direct descendants.

Mutiny on the High Seas

Set Sail, December 23, 1787

Captain William Bligh set sail from Spithead, England on the HMS *Bounty*. The mission was to get breadfruit plants from Tahiti. British slave owners wanted the plants to feed their slaves in Jamaica.

But the *Bounty* was a small ship. Bligh thought the ship was not big enough to haul such a large cargo. The ship was overcrowded. It would only get worse.

Life at Sea

Captain Bligh was mean. He yelled at his men. He had a bad temper. But he was a good captain.

He did not want his men to get sick. Many sailors got scurvy at sea. Bligh knew that eating sauerkraut would keep them well. He made sure the crew ate a lot of it—YUCK!

The ship ran into bad storms and could not sail around Cape Horn at the tip of South America. Instead they sailed around the Cape of Good Hope at the tip of Africa. This route made for a longer voyage.

Arrive in Paradise, October 26, 1788

After 10 months at sea, the men arrived in Tahiti. They were very happy. But the crew could not leave right away. The plants were not ready. The men had to wait for the breadfruit plants to grow before they could transport them. The *Bounty* stayed in Tahiti for six months!

The island seemed like paradise to the crew. Many of the men fell in love with the women on the island. The men grew lazy and did not want to work. They wanted to stay on the island forever.

Leave Paradise, April 4, 1789

Life on the *Bounty* was worse when it left Tahiti. The ship was full of breadfruit shoots—young trees that were bound for the Caribbean where they were to be planted. Bligh even gave up his captain's rooms to hold them all.

The men felt overcrowded. They missed the Tahitian women. They were angry with Bligh for making them leave. And the plants needed water. Bligh rationed the crew's drinking water so there was enough for the thirsty young plants.

Mutiny, April 18, 1789

Early on April 18, 1789, the crew dragged Bligh on deck with his hands tied. He was still in his pajamas! Fletcher Christian led most of the *Bounty*'s crew in a mutiny against Captain William Bligh.

Captain Bligh and 18 others were set adrift in a 23-foot boat. The mutineers threw breadfruit at them and called the captain "Breadfruit Bligh."

Alone at Sea

Captain Bligh might have been a poor leader, but he was a great sailor. He brought the boat safely to a tiny island called Tofoa.

It was a hostile island. Bligh lost one man, John Norton, to the natives before escaping back to the sea with the rest of his crew.

Bligh soon realized he had to change course. He had only enough food for the 18 men for five days. Bligh made the supplies last for 48 days at sea. He rationed the food. No one died of starvation or thirst on the voyage.

Return to England

After seven weeks adrift at sea, Bligh traveled on to the island of Timor, and then returned safely to England. He faced a trial there for the loss of his ship and crew. He was found not guilty.

Pitcairn Island, January 15, 1790

The mutineers returned to Tahiti. But Fletcher Christian feared it was not safe. He knew Bligh was an excellent sailor. Bligh would tell the British what happened. He knew a ship would search for them.

Christian and eight other mutineers took six Tahitian men and 12 women to find a new island. They found tiny Pitcairn Island. This was their new home.

On January 23, 1790, Christian's men burned the *Bounty* to destroy any trace of the mutiny.

Trouble in Paradise

But life was not perfect on the island. On September 20, 1793, five of the mutineers and all of the Polynesian men killed each other in a jealous massacre.

Over the next seven years, the Polynesian women killed most of the remaining mutineers. Only one mutineer, John Adams, survived. He became the leader of the island and lived there for almost 40 years.

The Wreck of the Essex
DATAFILE

Timeline

November 1820

A sperm whale strikes the *Essex* twice.

February 1821

The remaining survivors of the wreck are rescued from two whaling boats.

Where Did Captain Pollard Sail?

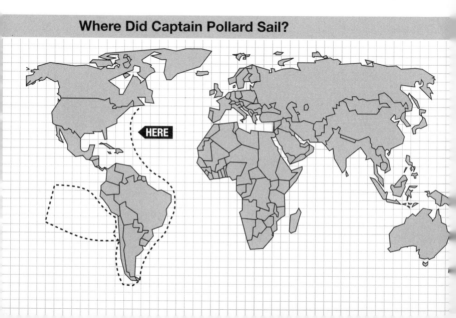

Key Terms

cannibals—people who eat other human beings

hoard—to gather and save something beyond one's need

keeled over—turned upside down or over on its side so that the keel shows

whaleboat—20-foot-long boat that mounts to the side of a larger ship; built for speed to chase whales

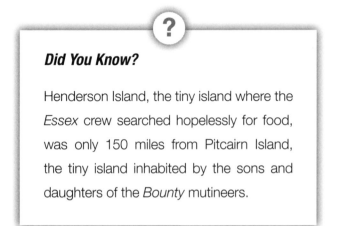

Did You Know?

Henderson Island, the tiny island where the *Essex* crew searched hopelessly for food, was only 150 miles from Pitcairn Island, the tiny island inhabited by the sons and daughters of the *Bounty* mutineers.

The Wreck of the Essex

August 12, 1819

The *Essex* was an old ship. People thought the *Essex* was a lucky ship because she had survived so many voyages. For the first year of her final voyage, she was lucky. The sailors caught many whales and turtles. They enjoyed the tasty food at sea.

Luck Runs Out, November 1820

All three whaleboats were on the hunt away from the *Essex*. One boat, led by First Mate Owen Chase, sprung a leak. Chase went back to the *Essex* with his crew to fix it.

While mending the whaleboat on the deck, Chase saw a sperm whale nearby. It was 100 feet away from the ship.

Suddenly, the whale charged the *Essex* head on. Chase and his crew were thrown off their feet. They were shocked. No one had ever heard of a whale attacking a boat before. Before they knew it, the whale was charging them again.

The crew quickly grabbed what they could and got back into the whaling boat. Within 10 minutes, the *Essex* had keeled over! When the other whale-boats returned, Captain Pollard and the crew could not believe the ship was floating on its side with its sails in the water.

The *Essex* Sinks Again

The men went to work to get the ship upright. They cut off the masts and most of the ship came up out of the water. After 45 minutes, they got the *Essex* upright. The crew took more food, water, turtles, and navigation tools from the ship. They even rigged her sails to use on the whaleboats. After two days, the men sailed away from the *Essex*. It sank as they looked back.

Lost at Sea

The men set sail in the whaling boats with little hope. They knew they were close to the Tahitian Islands. But they were afraid they were not safe. The crew believed that cannibals lived on the Tahitian islands. They headed for Easter Island instead. They thought the journey would take about two months. In the end, the crew would spend three months adrift at sea!

Sperm Whale Facts

- Largest brain and head size of any animal

- Layer of blubber is 4–12 inches thick

- Single s-shaped blowhole is 20 inches long

- Males are 50–60 feet long and weigh 40–50 tons

- Named for the oil it produces in the spermaceti organ in its head

- Eats giant squid, octopus, and other sea creatures

- Forms strong bonds with other pod members and protects others

- Deepest diving of all whales

- Swims up to 27 miles per hour

- Life expectancy of more than 70 years

Land in Sight! December 20, 1820

After less than a month at sea, the crew saw Henderson Island. The men searched for fresh water on the island. It took several days before they found any water. But they could only get to it when the tide was low. They ate almost every living plant, bird, and egg on the island.

After five days, the crew realized that there was not enough food for them to survive. They took as much water as they could, and headed back to sea. Three men chose to stay on the island.

Back to Sea, December 25, 1820

The crew were so weak when they left the island, they could no longer navigate. The men just lay in the boats. A storm blew up and the three boats were separated. One boat was never seen again.

Each of the two surviving crews faced another horror. On Owen Chase's boat, two men, Matthew Joy and Isaac Cole, died. When Isaac Cole died, Chase decided they should eat the body so they could survive. The men struggled with the decision. They knew they would die soon if they did not eat anything. They ate Cole's body.

Captain Pollard's crew faced the same problem. The men drew sticks to see who would be the first eaten. The man with the shortest stick lost.

This man was 17-year-old Owen Coffin, the captain's nephew. The captain begged to be eaten instead. But Coffin would not allow it. The man with the second shortest stick, Charles Ramsdell, had to shoot Coffin.

Ramsdell begged Coffin to shoot him instead. It was a horrible choice, but the men knew that they would die if they did not eat someone. Ramsdell shot Coffin. All of the crew, except Captain Pollard who could not eat his own nephew, ate him.

Rescue at Last

On February 18, 1821, the crew of the British ship the *Indian* rescued the three remaining men in Owen Chase's boat: Owen Chase, Benjamin Lawrence, and Thomas Nickerson. Captain Pollard's boat was discovered five days later by the crew of the whaling ship the *Dauphin*. Only two men were still alive in Pollard's boat: Captain Pollard and Charles Ramsdell.

The five men had traveled about 3,500 miles during 90 to 95 days at sea. The three men on Henderson Island were also rescued.

Aftermath

Captain Pollard went on to become the captain of the *Two Brothers* in 1821. When it wrecked, he felt ruined. Pollard never returned to the sea.

Owen Chase wrote a book called *The Wreck of the Whaleship Essex*. In later years, Chase's son, William, was on a whaling ship in the South Pacific. He met a young whaler, Herman Melville, who was very interested in his father's story. Owen Chase's book became the inspiration for Melville's famous book, *Moby Dick*.

Owen Chase lived to be an old man. But he suffered from terrible headaches. In the end, he lost his mind and hoarded crackers in his attic. Like Pollard, Owen Chase never really got over the wreck of the *Essex*.

The Lusitania *Caught Off Guard*

DATAFILE

Timeline

August 1914
Britain declares war on Germany. World War I begins.

May 1915
Germans sink the *Lusitania*.

April 1917
America enters World War I.

Where Did Captain Turner Sail?

Key Terms

munitions—weapons, explosives, and ammunition used in warfare

recluse—someone who avoids or hides from other people

scapegoat—a person who takes the blame for an incident, who may or may not be guilty

U-Boat—a German submarine used in warfare

?

Did You Know?

April 22, 1915, right next to a newspaper advertisement for the *Lusitania* voyage was a warning from the German Embassy. It stated that anyone sailing through a war zone did so at his or her own risk. The *Lusitania* did just that.

The Lusitania *Caught Off Guard*

The Unsinkable Ship

The *Lusitania* was a British luxury ship. It took people to and from England and America on vacation. There were restaurants, musicians, a library, and beautiful rooms for the wealthy passengers. People called it a "floating palace."

Everyone thought the *Lusitania* was safe during World War I because it could sail faster than any submarine. Subs could not sink what they could not catch.

Submarines were a great danger to ships. They moved under the water. They could sneak up on ships. They could launch torpedoes at them.

But it was against the rules of war to attack a passenger ship. The *Lusitania* had even sailed through a war zone during the early part of World War I. So, no one thought the Germans would sink the *Lusitania* in less than 20 minutes!

Set Sail, May 1, 1915

The *Lusitania* was ready to sail from New York to England. The ship was loaded with passengers and goods. Today, many people suspect that it was also loaded with munitions. It was against American and international law for a passenger ship to transport weapons. Some thought it was the perfect way to disguise the shipment and arm the British.

While checking over the ship, the Master at Arms found three Germans hiding on board. He took a camera from them. He locked them in the ship's jail cells. No one knows for sure who they were or if they were really spies. The *Lusitania* would never arrive in England where they were to face trial. They did not live to be identified or to tell their story.

Bowler Bill

Captain Turner was a great seaman. Known as "Bowler Bill" for the hat that he always wore, Turner had a history of saving crews from shipwrecks. He often took big risks to help others. Turner had once steered his own ship into a storm to rescue the crew of a sinking ship.

Dangerous Waters

Captain Turner decided not to use one of the *Lusitania*'s boiler rooms in order to save coal for the war. With only 19 out of 25 boilers in use, the ship could not go at top speed.

On the sixth day of the journey, the *Lusitania* was off the coast of southern Ireland. Due to fog, Turner ordered that the ship slow down. He was expecting another armed ship, the HMS *Juno*, to escort the *Lusitania* through the war zone. The *Juno* never came.

Rather than zigzagging the *Lusitania*, Turner ordered the ship to go straight through the waters. This broke British orders. Zigzagging was meant to make it harder for subs to shoot a large ship. Turner thought this was a waste of time and fuel.

May 7, 1915, "Fateful Friday"

Just after 11:00 a.m., Turner got a coded message from Vice Admiral Coke. Because it was in code, Turner could not read it on deck. He went to his cabin to decipher the message.

While he was working on the first message, Turner got another message from Coke. This one was not in code. It warned him of a German sub nearby. Turner quickly changed the ship's course. He turned the *Lusitania* sharply. People fell over due to the sharp turn.

"Submarine Active in Southern part of Irish Channel . . . Make certain Lusitania *gets this." — Vice Admiral Coke*

At 12:40 p.m. Turner got another message from Coke. It told him that British forces had seen a submarine in the area. Turner believed that the sub was moving in the other direction. He thought the *Lusitania* was out of danger.

At 1:40 p.m. Turner recognized a lighthouse on the Irish coast. It was the Old Head of Kinsale. Turner steered the *Lusitania* toward Queenstown, Ireland. Turner now felt the ship was safe. He then left a junior officer in charge and went to his cabin. This was a deadly mistake. A German U-Boat had found them. Then it fired a torpedo.

At 2:10 p.m. Turner heard what sounded like a big door slamming. A torpedo had struck the *Lusitania*!

A second explosion followed. This was much larger and more deadly. It was not a torpedo. It might have been the alleged hidden munitions exploding. It might have been a reaction between the coal and the oxygen in the *Lusitania*'s empty boiler chamber. Today, people still argue about what caused the second explosion.

Panic!

The *Lusitania* tilted to one side as it sunk into the ocean. This meant that half of the lifeboats hanging on the higher side were useless. Captain Turner ordered that no one get into the lifeboats on the lower side until they were closer to the water. But the passengers panicked. They began cutting the boats down. People jumped the distance of many stories down onto the lifeboats below. Many people died from the fall. The falling boats also crushed people standing on the deck.

Within 18 minutes of the torpedo strike, the *Lusitania* sank. More than 1,100 men, women, and children died in the wreck. This number included more than 120 Americans and the three Germans who were locked in the jail cells.

After the Wreck

Captain Turner, along with hundreds of others, survived the wreck. Small fishing boats from Ireland rescued them. The *Flying Fish* was a steamboat that made several trips back and forth to rescue the victims. Captain Thomas Brierley of the *Flying Fish* was so upset by the incident that he asked to be buried at sea by the *Lusitania* wreck site.

Turner was a scapegoat for the tragedy. The British government accused him of being reckless, sailing too slowly, and not zigzagging.

The British Admiralty cleared Turner of any blame. But he lived the rest of his life as a recluse.

The *Lusitania* tilted to one side as it sank.

Nautical Alphabet

BST	British Summer Time
C	Celsius
CG	Coast Guard
E	East
ETA	Estimated Time of Arrival
F	Fahrenheit
GMT	Greenwich Mean Time
HMS	His/Her Majesty's Ship
HW	High Water
LW	Low Water
N	North
R	Rocky
S	South
SOS	Save Our Ship
SS	Steam Ship
W	West
Wk	Wreck

CHAPTER 4

SS St. Louis *Turned Away*
DATAFILE

Timeline

October 1929

The Great Depression begins.

June 1939

SS *St. Louis* is turned away from Cuba.

September 1939

World War II begins.

Where Did Captain Schroeder Sail?

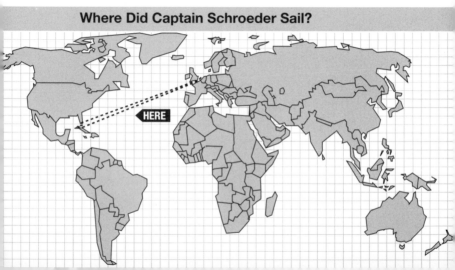

Key Terms

concentration camp—a Nazi prison where many people were tortured and killed

Nazi—a German government party led by Adolph Hitler

refugee—someone who leaves his or her homeland in search of a better place

?

Did You Know?

For the first time in more than 200 years, during the years 1932–1938, more people left the United States than came to the United States.

SS St. Louis *Turned Away*

Set Sail, May 13, 1939

The SS *St. Louis* was a luxury ship. It had swimming pools, movie theaters, and plenty of fine food. Its mission in May of 1939 was to deliver Jewish refugees to Cuba. These people were trying to escape from the Nazis in Germany. Some had suffered in Nazi prison camps. They wanted to start a new life.

The passengers on the ship paid a high price to board. Many Jews had lost their life savings to the Germans. Families scraped money together to send only one person to freedom. Others got money from relatives in other countries.

The captain of the
SS *St. Louis*,
Captain Gustav Schroeder

The passengers were nervous boarding the *St. Louis*. Some came out of hiding to travel. They were afraid they would be tricked and sent to a concentration camp. The ship was German owned. It flew the Nazi flag. It had a large portrait of Adolph Hitler on board.

Captain Gustav Schroeder knew the passengers' fear. He ordered that the crew treat them well. He took special care to make it a pleasant voyage. He even formed passenger committees to help ease their fears. He wanted to save the passengers from the Nazis.

Bad Signs

The *St. Louis* had been at sea only a half hour when Captain Schroeder got a message from the Marine Superintendent of the shipping line. The *St. Louis* should hurry to Cuba. Two other boats full of Jewish refugees were heading there, too. The captain feared his passengers would not be welcome in Cuba. His instinct was right!

On May 23, an elderly passenger, Moritz Weiler, died on board. Captain Schroeder feared that the passengers would see this as a bad sign. He decided to bury the body at sea that night. This way, the passengers might not find out.

Evil Plans

Captain Schroeder did not know that one crew member, Otto Schiendick, was a courier for the

German Secret Police. His mission was to get secret documents about the United States from a spy in Cuba.

Schiendick did not like the Jews. He sang Nazi songs and upset the passengers. He even tried to persuade the Captain that Weiler should be wrapped in a Nazi swastika flag. Captain Schroeder did not agree.

Joseph Goebbels also worked for the Nazis. He told the Cubans that the passengers on the *St. Louis* were criminals. He wanted the Cubans to reject the Jews. He did not want any country to help the Jews.

When the *St. Louis* arrived, the Cubans were afraid of the passengers. They thought the Jews were criminals who would take their jobs.

Manuel Benitez was a corrupt Cuban official. He sold permits to the Jews for them to land in Cuba. The president of Cuba found out that Benitez was getting rich from these permits.

On May 5, 1939, before the *St. Louis* even left Germany, Cuban President Bru passed Decree 937. It made the permits illegal. The passengers never had permission to land in Cuba!

May 27, 1939, Arrival in Cuba

Near Cuba, Captain Schroeder got a notice that he would have to anchor off shore. Cuban officials boarded the ship. They did not tell the Captain why. The passengers were very scared. They thought they would be sent to concentration camps.

Friends and family who were already in Cuba rented boats. They circled the *St. Louis* and waved to the passengers.

Jewish refugees aboard the SS *St. Louis* look out a port hole.

No one was allowed to leave the *St. Louis*. Even the crew was not allowed on shore. This was a problem for Otto Schiendick. He wanted to get the secret documents from Robert Hoffman, a German spy working in Cuba.

Hoffman worked as a German official with Luis Clasing. But Clasing was not a German spy. Clasing was busy negotiating with President Bru about the passengers, so he allowed Hoffman to take his place and board the *St. Louis* to speak with Captain Schroeder.

Before he boarded, Hoffman hid secret documents in pens, a cane, and magazines. But Hoffman was not allowed to bring anything on board with him. He then persuaded Captain Schroeder to allow the crew to go ashore. There he was able to pass the documents to Schiendick.

Schiendick wanted to return to Europe quickly. He did not care about the Jewish passengers. He only wanted to get the documents back to the Nazis. Schiendick would have been in great danger if he were caught with the documents!

Nowhere to Go

The *St. Louis* circled Cuba for one week. The passengers were not allowed to land in Cuba or the United States. The Cuban government wanted more money to allow them to land.

The US government did not help the passengers. They were not invited to land in America. In fact, the Coast Guard is rumored to have shot at the ship. Officially, the Coast Guard had orders to follow the *St. Louis* in case America changed its policy and allowed the ship to land. The Coast Guard never received word to accept the refugees.

Finally, President Bru of Cuba decided he would not allow the *St. Louis* to land. On June 2, 1939, the ship was forced to leave the Cuban harbor. Captain Schroeder had no choice but to return to Europe.

Desperation!

The St. Louis was running low on food and supplies. The ship had to speed toward Europe. But it had nowhere to go! Germany did not want the Jews back. The Jews did not want to go back, either! They were afraid they would be sent to concentration camps.

Captain Schroeder used passenger committees to watch for problems. They patrolled the decks. The captain feared mass suicides or a mutiny.

A passenger named Aaron Pozner, who had spent time in a concentration camp, led a small mutiny. He did not want to go back to Germany. Captain Schroeder was able to control the passengers and crew. They stayed on course.

Finally, Captain Schroeder learned that four countries would take the Jewish passengers. From June 16–20, the passengers left the *St. Louis*. Holland took 181 refugees. France took 224. Great Britain took 228, and Belgium took 214.

Sadly, Germany conquered three of these four nations in the coming years of World War II. Only those sent to Great Britain were spared the ultimate abuse and return to Nazi terror. Many died in concentration camps.

A family on the deck of the SS *St. Louis*

Boat People Stranded at Sea
DATAFILE

Timeline

April 1975

South Vietnam falls to Communist rule.

January 1996

The United Nations stops funding refugee camps.

March 1996

Vietnam agrees to take back the boat people.

Where is Vietnam?

HERE

Key Terms

boat people—refugees who flee their country in boats

Communism—a system of government in which a single political party controls property, including goods and businesses, which are all owned by the state

Communist—a person who supports Communism; an organization that follows Communist ideas

repatriate—a refugee who returns to his or her homeland to live

?

Did You Know?

Pirates are not extinct. They exist to this day. Real-life pirates still terrorize the high seas around the world, stealing from ships and harming people on board.

Boat People Stranded at Sea

1975, The End of the War

War is a terrible thing. When the Vietnam War ended in 1975, many people there were afraid. The new government was Communist. Many Vietnamese did not agree with the Communist leaders' ideas. They were in great danger if they stayed.

The choice to leave was a painful one. Vietnam was their homeland. They had loved ones who stayed behind. Many people had little or no money. They did not know what the future would bring. They did not know where they would go. They risked everything to escape.

Vietnamese people fleeing their homeland in a small, overcrowded fishing boat.

Shipping Out

The Vietnamese boat people did not have time to build strong ships. They did not have proper supplies, equipment, or food. They had to escape in secret.

The boat people often escaped in fishing boats. The boats were not built to endure the rough waters of the high seas. They offered little protection from storms. People crammed into them. Sinking or falling overboard were real threats.

The boats often left at night, crowded and poorly suited for the sea. Once at sea, the boat people did not have anywhere to go. They hoped that wherever they landed, perhaps Thailand, Malaysia, or Hong Kong, life would be better than it was in Vietnam.

Piracy!

Thai pirates often attacked the boat people. They tortured and abused them. The pirates sometimes abducted the Vietnamese women.

This would be a horrible event in any culture, but it was especially so for the Vietnamese. In the traditional Vietnamese culture, the man is the head of his family. The abduction and torture of the Vietnamese women upset the men in the boats. They tried to protect their women by fighting the pirates. But they did not have the weapons to match the pirates. The Vietnamese men often died or were tortured for trying to defend their families.

Stranded at Sea

The boat people suffered in many other ways. The United Nations (UN) believes one-third of all the boat people died at sea. Storms often tossed their tiny fishing boats, drowning all aboard.

Many others died of dehydration and starvation. The boats were overloaded, and the refugees did not have the supplies they needed to survive a great voyage.

Koh Kra Island

Stranded at sea, the refugees hoped to find a better place. This, however, was not what many found. Pirates took some refugees to Koh Kra Island.

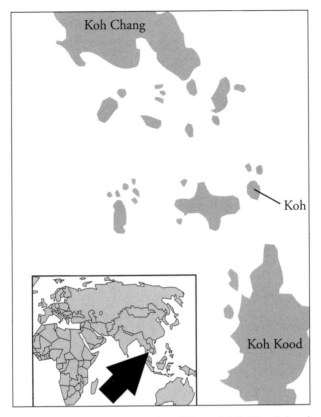

Koh Chang

Koh

Koh Kood

Life at sea was bad, but life on Koh Kra Island was even worse. The pirates treated the boat people horribly. Women were tortured. The pirates made the women stand in seawater for hours while crabs ate their flesh. During one 12-month period, more than 160 refugees died on Koh Kra Island.

By 1977, word had spread about the Thai pirates. Many boat people headed for Malaysia to avoid the pirates. This route took much longer. Many more refugees died at sea due to the length of the voyage.

The boat people also traveled to Hong Kong. The people of Hong Kong soon began to suffer from what is called "compassion fatigue." They did not want the boat people to come to Hong Kong. The boat people overcrowded the city and took jobs away from the residents. There was little food and housing. The city was not prepared to house and feed so many people all at once.

Between 1975 and 1992, more than 210,000 boat people escaped to Hong Kong. Hong Kong tried to force the boat people to repatriate. But the boat people did not want to return to Vietnam. Rioting and fighting broke out often between the people of Hong Kong and the Vietnamese refugees.

SOS

In March 1979, a tiny boat left Vietnam. More than 500 people were crammed on it. The boat people were crowded and hungry. But the boat could not hold them all. While out at sea, the boat's hull cracked. All 500 of the refugees jumped into the water. Most died, but one boy fought for his life. His name was Nguyen Dinh Thang.

Nguyen Dinh Thang survived and decided to help his people. He found a new home in the United States.

In 1981, he started an organization called "Boat People SOS." This group helps Vietnamese boat people with immigration, health, education, and family reunion issues.

Help for the Weary

In the late 1970s, the UN decided to help the boat people. It set up refugee camps in Hong Kong, Thailand, Indonesia, Malaysia, and the Philippines.

In the late 1980s, some Vietnamese decided to return home. They missed loved ones too much. By the late 1990s, almost 57,000 boat people had returned to Vietnam.

But many others did not want to return to Vietnam. The government was still Communist.

In January 1996, the UN stopped funding the refugee camps. Now the remaining boat people had to return to Vietnam if they could not look after themselves. In 1996, more than 40,000 boat people lived in UN refugee camps.

Finally in March 1996, the Vietnamese government allowed the boat people to come back home.

No Place Like Home?

The Vietnam that the boat people returned to was not as it used to be. Many had no family left in Vietnam. They had no property anymore. The Vietnamese people who had stayed often rejected the repatriates. The boat people were scarred and damaged from the horrors they had survived.

Abby Sunderland

DATAFILE

Timeline

July 16, 2009

After 13 months and two days, Zac Sunderland becomes the youngest person to sail solo around the world.

January 23, 2010

Abby Sunderland leaves Marina del Rey, California, to begin her attempt to become the youngest person to sail solo around the world.

Where is Marina del Rey, California?

HERE

Key Terms

beacon—a fire or light set up in a high or prominent position as a warning, signal, or celebration

legs—a section or part of a journey or course

plaque—a thin, flat plate or tablet of metal, porcelain, etc., intended for ornament, as on a wall

?

Did You Know?

The Jules Verne Trophy was first awarded to the yacht that sailed around the world in 80 days. The prize is now awarded to the fastest yacht and crew to circumnavigate the globe. The current holder smashed the previous record by over two days. The trip took just over 45 days.

Abby Sunderland

Abby Sunderland, 16, hoped to become the youngest person to circumnavigate the globe alone. She intended to sail all the way around the world by herself. But she didn't quite make it.

Due to equipment problems on her sailing yacht, Abby was stranded at sea. An enormous wave had broken her sailboat's mast. That's what holds up the sails.

A French fishing boat rescued Abby in the Indian Ocean. Her damaged boat, the *Wild Eyes,* had to be abandoned. It was too far out at sea to be towed to land.

Zac, Abby's older brother, was the first person under 18 to sail around the world solo. He was 17 when he set the record in 2009. Zac received a plaque from Arnold Schwarzenegger. He was the governor of California at the time.

Only a little over a month later, Zac's record was broken. A younger British sailor named Mike Perham completed the trip, beating Zac's record.

Jessica Watson of Australia was even younger than Mike. She completed the trip in May 2010, just three days shy of her 17th birthday.

In 2012, Laura Dekker of Holland sailed around the world too. She was 16 years and 123 days old when she finished. So far she is the youngest to make the trip.

Abby is the second of eight children in the Sunderland family. They are an enthusiastic boating family that sails all over. They have sailed in Australia, New Zealand, the United Kingdom, Mexico, and other areas. The Sunderlands are devout Christians. All eight kids are homeschooled.

Abby started preparing for her journey at age 13. Her father and other sailors taught her the ropes. She learned to handle an ocean boat all on her own. Abby was very determined.

Her 40-foot sailboat was a was a sloop—a single-masted sailboat—called the *Wild Eyes*. It was painted in bright yellows and reds. On the back were painted two catlike green eyes. The *Wild Eyes*

had been built in 2001 by a company in Australia. It was made specifically for sailing solo. It was fast and agile.

Abby's trip started off at Marina del Rey, California. The date was January 23, 2010.

There hadn't been enough time to do a full test run. That would have included several days in different conditions. So the team decided she should go ahead. She could stop in Cabo San Lucas if she needed to. This port city is in the Mexican state of Baja California Sur.

It turned out she *did* need to stop there. Her wind generators and solar panels weren't working well enough. She had to use her diesel engine more than planned. She was having some electrical problems too. So she had to stop in Cabo and get her boat worked on.

On February 6, 2010, Abby's boat was ready to go. She restarted her attempt to sail around the world. Her plan was to make an unassisted, non-stop, solo circumnavigation in ten legs. She would start at Cabo and return there after going around the world. On February 19, she crossed the equator into the South Pacific.

There was a big earthquake and tsunami in Chile on February 27. People were concerned for Abby's safety. But she was out in deep water, so she didn't feel it.

On March 31, she sailed around Cape Horn. That's the southernmost tip of South America. Abby was the youngest sailor ever to do so. Cape Horn is known for its bad weather. She came up against some rough waves and wind as she got close. But then everything smoothed out.

When Abby got to Cape Town, South Africa, she had to stop. It was April 24. Her autopilot system needed to be repaired. That ended her nonstop attempt. But she planned to continue her circumnavigation.

Abby left Cape Town on May 21. It was looking like she wouldn't be back to Cabo until August or September.

Then, on the morning of June 10, she experienced some high winds. Her boat was knocked over a few times, but she got it righted and kept going. She was in a remote area of the Indian Ocean. It was about 2,000 miles west of Australia.

Abby lost contact with her father and the rest of the team. Her satellite phone had stopped working. She was in trouble. About an hour later her two emergency radio beacons came on. That alerted authorities that she was in distress. The nearest vessel was 400 miles away.

The next morning Australian authorities sent a plane. It flew out to where Abby was. Her mast was broken. That's why the satellite phone stopped working.

Abby was rescued by a French fishing ship *Ile de la Reunion.*

"She got out of her vessel with the clothes on her back," her father told reporters.

Somali Pirates
DATAFILE

Timeline

October 18, 2005

The cargo ship *Panagia* is captured by pirates off the coast of Somalia. A ransom of $700 thousand is demanded for the return of the ship, its cargo of coal, and the crew.

October 28, 2007

Somali pirates capture the *Golden Nori*, a Japanese chemical tanker ship, and demand a ransom.

Where is Somalia?

HERE

Key Terms

pirate—a person who attacks and robs ships at sea

ransom—a sum of money or other payment demanded or paid for the release of a prisoner

stimulant—a substance that raises levels of physiological or nervous activity in the body

warlord—a person with power who has both military and civil control over an area

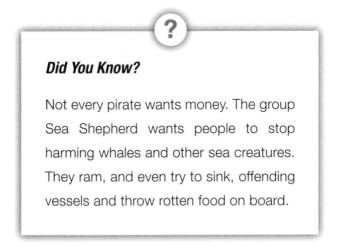

Did You Know?

Not every pirate wants money. The group Sea Shepherd wants people to stop harming whales and other sea creatures. They ram, and even try to sink, offending vessels and throw rotten food on board.

Somali Pirates

Pirates of old said things like "Aye, matey." They used swords and cannons to hijack ships. When cornered, they buried their treasure on deserted islands. They came back for it later—if they were still alive. And if they took hostages, they made them into galley slaves.

Today's pirates operate a little differently. They still hijack ships. But modern pirates use machine guns and smart phones with GPS. They travel in small, fast boats with only three or four pirates aboard. And most of them do their pirating around what is known as the Horn of Africa where Somalia is located.

Somali pirates don't generally steal the cargo. That's what the pirates of old did. Today, they take over ships large and small. Then they charge a ransom. The more valuable the cargo, the higher the ransom. Once the ransom is paid, they release the ship and take off. Somali pirates made about $146 million in ransoms in 2011 alone.

Once they overpower a ship, they take it to a nearby island. They let the company who owns the ship know their demands. Typically they ask for as much as $10 to $20 million. But they will settle for $2 to $5 million. Often the negotiations, or discussions, take months. The pirates keep the people or crew aboard hostage until the ransom is paid.

Until recently, they treat their hostages pretty well. They fed them and didn't abuse them. But lately that has started to change. Some pirates have started chopping off hostages' hands or feet. They do that if the ransom isn't paid quickly enough.

Pirates in Somalia are kind of like an organized crime group. They drive expensive cars and live in fancy houses. They pay off officials to keep things running smoothly.

In Somalia, pirates are about the only ones making money. Right next to fancy homes are tin shacks. Children are starving. There are few jobs. Shootings and kidnappings happen often.

Somalia is a country at war. It is on the east coast of Africa, below the Arabian Peninsula. The area is known as the Horn of Africa because of its shape. It juts out into the Arabian Sea and the Indian Ocean.

Somalia's civil war started in 1991. Former president Mohamed Siad Barre was kicked out. The country was in chaos. Basically, there was no government.

Since there was no government, there was no navy. No one was protecting the country's coastline. Fishermen from other countries started fishing around Somalia. There was no one to stop them. Also, big companies started illegally dumping toxic waste. They were killing off the fish.

In Somalia, fishermen are worse off than herders or factory workers. But before the civil war began, they were at least able to make a living. That all changed in the early 1990s.

The Somali fishermen were tired of foreigners stealing their fish. And they were sick of big companies killing the fish with their pollution. They decided to do something. Many of them turned to piracy.

In the beginning they acted as a sort of informal coast guard. They patrolled the waters around Somalia. But then they discovered they could make money by using violence. Somali warlords caught on too. They started financing the pirates.

Pirates usually demand to get paid in US $100 bills. One Somali pirate told how the loot is usually split up. Farah Ismail Eid is in prison for 15 years. He told a reporter how it all works.

Members of the US Coast Guard Law Enforcement Detachment and Combined Task Force 151's board, search, and seizure team, prepare to search a suspicious *dhow*.

A dhow is a type of sailing vessel with one or more masts with triangular sails used in the Red Sea and Indian Ocean.

"Believe me, a lot of our money has gone straight into the government's pockets," Eid said. Their bosses usually get 20 percent. The pirates set aside another 20 percent for future raids. That money covers things like guns, gas, and cigarettes. Government officials get 30 percent. And the remaining 30 percent is split up among the pirates who hijack the ship.

So, the pirates get 50 percent, while 50 percent goes to other people.

Most pirates are teenage boys when they start out because there are almost no other jobs. They are promised easy money. Often they are using a drug called *khat,* which is a kind of stimulant. It gives them energy and makes them unpredictable. Pirating is a dangerous profession. Many are killed while still in their teens.

One well-known hijacking took place in 2009 near Somalia. An American ship, the *Maersk*

Alabama, was captured by pirates. US Navy SEALs shot the captors and saved the day. A movie is being made about the five-day standoff. It will star Tom Hanks.

Shipping companies are cracking down on Somali pirates. Many ships now have barbed wire on them. That helps keep pirates from boarding. High-pressure hoses are also used. The water knocks them off when they try to board.

Governments, too, are trying to stop Somali piracy. China, Russia, the United States, and other nations are actively working to shut the pirates down.

Amanda Thorns
DATAFILE

Timeline

November 6, 2010

On a sailboat called the *Emma Goldman*, Amanda Thorns sets off from Martha's Vineyard, Massachusetts, to the Virgin Islands with her father Willie and boat owner Dennis White.

November 9, 2010

Massive 30-foot waves slam into the *Emma Goldman* causing it to roll 360-degrees.

Where is Martha's Vineyard, Massachusetts?

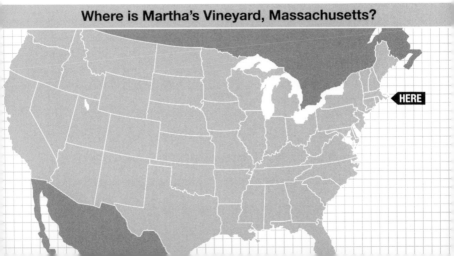

HERE

Key Terms

gale—a very strong wind

ketch—a sailboat with two masts

ordeal—any extremely severe or trying test, experience, or trial

rigged—to assemble, install, or prepare

?

Did You Know?

The island of Martha's Vineyard is seven miles off the coast of Massachusetts. Its winter population is 15,000 but swells to over 100,000 during the summer.

CHAPTER 8

Amanda Thorns

"Just to have a sunny vacation and spend time with Dad." That's all Amanda Thorns wanted. Instead, her next 15 days were a hellish ordeal at sea.

After three days, her father was killed in a bad storm with huge waves. And for the next 12 days, Amanda and the boat's captain were stranded. The sailboat's mast was broken, so they couldn't get any wind to move forward.

They were out in the middle of the Atlantic Ocean. And the boat was not equipped with an Emergency Position Indicating Radio Beacon (EPIRB). That's a device that sends out a signal to other boats. It lets them know when someone is in trouble.

The radio was damaged and didn't work, so they couldn't call for help. So no one even knew they were missing. They wouldn't have been able to find the boat to come get them, anyway.

Amanda, 25, grew up in Knoxville, Tennessee. She moved to New Orleans for the live music and swing dancing. But when her father asked if she wanted to sail to the Caribbean, she jumped at the chance. She didn't get to see him all that often.

Amanda quit her waitress job in New Orleans and headed north to Cape Cod, Massachusetts. Her father lived there in the seaside resort island of Martha's Vineyard.

The trip started off on November 6, 2010. It was a Saturday. Amanda and her father were on a sailboat called the *Emma Goldman*. It was a sturdy wooden ketch, 41 feet long.

Captain Willie Thorns, Amanda's father, was an experienced sailor and carpenter. His best friend, Captain Dennis White, had built the boat. Like many sailors in New England, he wanted to take his

These sailboats and fishing boats are protected from the ravages of the sea by the harbor at Martha's Vineyard. Captain Dennis White lives in West Tisbury on the island.

boat south for the winter. The three of them were planning to get back to Massachusetts the first week of December.

"The weather maps that Dennis had printed out showed that they were going to be all right with the weather," Captain White's wife said. "And then this gale stopped right above them."

The gale was a Nor'easter—a really bad storm. It was the kind of ocean storm seen in the movie *The Perfect Storm.*

Amanda described the sound of the 30-foot waves hitting the boat. It was scary and loud. "It sounded like a bus hitting the side of the boat, over and over again."

On the third day, her father was on deck keeping watch. A monster wave hit. It rolled the boat upside down and over, in a 360-degree turn. When the mast went down into the water, it broke. The mast is the tall vertical pole that holds the sails.

Amanda and Captain White were in their bunks trying to sleep when it hit. They ran up to the deck. Amanda was in her pajamas. They saw her father in the water. He had been injured, and his face was bloody. He was caught in the ropes holding the sails.

Captain White made a decision to cut the ropes that entangled Captain Thorns in order to save him. But he also knew that Captain Thorns could be easily lost to the sea.

"I told him I loved him," Amanda said. "I kissed his forehead and his hand, and I said, 'Don't leave me here.'"

Just then another huge wave came up. It washed him away. Captain Willie Thorns's body was never found.

Many people would have given up at that point. But not Amanda.

"I wanted to sit down on the deck of the boat and cry and cry," she said. "But this other part of me that was bigger said, 'I don't want to die.'"

She and Dennis still had to ride out the storm. For the next three days they bailed water from the boat. The sailboat's damaged mast was in the water next to the hull. It was still connected by the ropes. The mast kept banging into the side of the boat. Dennis worried it would puncture the hull. But luckily, it didn't.

At one point the skies cleared. Waves were still hitting the boat, but the clouds were gone. Amanda could see the stars.

The storm cleared. But without sails, the boat couldn't move. Dennis made a new mast and sail from the lifeboat. It was much smaller, but it helped them move some. They traveled about 50 miles using the rigged sail.

Twice they saw ships pass in the distance. But they were too far away to get their attention, even with flares. Finally, after having been at sea for two weeks, they were rescued. A Greek freighter heading for Nigeria found them. Dennis and Amanda had sent up emergency flares when they realized the Greek ship was close enough to see them..

"Shipwrecked for 12 days," Amanda wrote on her Facebook page. "Rescued today by the Greek ship *Triathlon*. Drinking whiskey and coke with the crew. Bermuda bound. Heartbroken and alive. RIP Capt. Willie Thorns. Bravest, strongest daddy."

"I get peace knowing that my father died doing his very favorite thing, with his very favorite person," Amanda said. "That's sort of what I'm clinging to right now."

Glossary

beacon—a fire or light set up in a high or prominent position as a warning, signal, or celebration

boat people—refugees who flee their country in boats

breadfruit—a seedless, starchy fruit that looks and tastes like bread

cannibals—people who eat other human beings

concentration camp—a Nazi prison where many people were tortured and killed

gale—a very strong wind

hoard—to gather and save something beyond one's need

keeled over—turned upside down or over on its side so that the keel shows

ketch—a sailboat with two masts

legs—a section or part of a journey or course

munitions—weapons, explosives, and ammunition used in warfare

mutiny—an effort to overthrow a leader

ordeal—any extremely severe or trying test, experience, or trial

pirate—a person who attacks and robs ships at sea

plaque—a thin, flat plate or tablet of metal, porcelain, etc., intended for ornament, as on a wall

ransom—a sum of money or other payment demanded or paid for the release of a prisoner

ration—to limit the daily amount of food allowed for each person

recluse—someone who avoids or hides from other people

refugee—someone who leaves his or her homeland in search of a better place

repatriate—a refugee who returns to his or her homeland to live

replica—a copy or model of something

rigged—to assemble, install, or prepare

sauerkraut—cooked and pickled cabbage

scapegoat—a person who takes the blame for an incident, who may or may not be guilty

scurvy—a disease caused by lack of ascorbic acid, often found in fruit

stimulant—a substance that raises levels of physiological or nervous activity in the body

warlord—a person with power who has both military and civil control over an area

whaleboat—20-foot-long boat that mounts to the side of a larger ship; built for speed to chase whales

Index